In praise of this book:

"Tracy Foote's *My Potty Activity Book* is a clever way to sustain a child's interest in potty training. Designed to be used over a period of time, the book has enough coloring pages and simple exercises to last throughout the potty training period. Even better, it promotes dialogue between parent and child, the key to successful potty training. Children will recognize themselves in the delightfully fresh illustrations. Like all really good parenting books, *My Potty Activity Book* accommodates different parenting styles. Whether potty training is started early or late, parents will find support and right-on-target suggestions to see them through the process." **-Shelly Hitchings, owner of Ablebaby.com**

"A great help at an important time! Most projects in life are accomplished using several tools. *My Potty Activity Book* is a great tool for toilet training. This important part of child development finds each child adjusting at different speeds and with different attitudes. *Potty Activity* is terrific in that it gets a child interested by using a medium (drawing) which the child finds interesting and fun. By drawing and connecting lines and answering easy questions the child becomes familiar with toilet training in a non-threatening manner. The child gradually becomes educated in what steps are necessary to use the toilet. The book could easily have been titled Potty Helper. The special list of 45 Potty Tips is (alone) worth the price of the book!" **-James Brock, Reviewer, Amazon.com**

"At last - the perfect potty training guide for successful toilet training! This book fits nicely into daily parenting needs when and where small children are involved. The book particularly gives the reader ideas on what is available "out there". The book will give them what to use, how to use it, and what it looks like - which is a very important point. *My Potty Activity Book* is an excellent starting point to the whole toilet training process without forcing consumer purchase of a particular product. GOOD WORK!" **-Petr Skoda, designer of FlipnFlush.com potty seats**

The day will come where you will look at your child in amazement and with pride realizing something has clicked. Something has registered.

Your child has initiated - with no reminder - going to the potty.

My Potty Activity Book
+45 Toilet Training Tips

Written and Illustrated by Tracy A. Foote

Table of Contents

For
Jacqueline,
Erika and Nicholas

About the Author

Tracy Foote is the mother of three young children. She graduated from the NY Bronx High School of Science, attended the United States Air Force Academy and served overseas in Germany. As a parent, after roughly 11,000 diaper changes, she wanted something to expedite and ease the pressures of potty training (on both parent and child) while adding a little fun and humor.

From the Author

Parenthood has many challenges, one of which is potty training. The hands-on activities in this book invite children to explore toilet training through images, questions, and simple exercises. Especially useful for potty training, the book uses real faces of children for your child to identify with. Share the book together in a quiet environment and later enjoy it while sitting on the potty.

The easy to remove pages allow you to work a page at a time and later display your child's work on a wall to further show your praise and encouragement. As your child's first teacher, use this book to provide a positive learning experience, encourage imagination, and help expedite potty training success.

Third printing
Published by TracyTrends
Printed in the United States of America
Text Copyright © 2000, 2001, 2007 by Tracy Foote
Illustration Copyright © 2000, 2001, 2007 by Tracy Foote

Send all inquiries to:

TracyTrends
C/O T. Foote
27 West 86 St Suite 17B
New York, NY 10024
tracytrends@aol.com
http://www.TracyTrends.com/
ISBN 10: 0-9708226-0-X
ISBN 13: 978-09708226-0-4

Congratulations!
You have received your Potty Activity Book!
Place a date by things you can do as you complete this book.

My name is _____ Age: _____ Date Training Started: _____

Date	My Potty Progress Chart
	I have daily patterns when I go poop or pee pee in my diaper.
	I show an interest in the potty and in others using the toilet.
	I keep my diaper dry for periods of time: sometimes 1 or 2 hours.
	I received my new potty.
	I can partially dress myself because my clothes are easy to take on and off.
	I can tell the difference between wet and dry.
	I sat on the potty with my clothes on to see how it feels.
	I can turn the sink water on and off.
	I can wash my hands with soap at the sink.
	I can dry my hands on a towel.
	I can put the lid and seat up or down if needed.
	I watched someone go potty.
	I can pull my underwear or training pants down by myself.
	I can sit on the potty with a bare bottom.
	I can read books while sitting on the potty.
	I taught my animal or doll how to go potty and wash hands.
	I did my first pee in the potty today!
	I remember to flush the toilet.
	I can help shop for toilet paper.

Dynamite!
You are doing great!

My name is _____ Age: ___ Date Training Completed: _____

Date	My Potty Progress Chart
	I did my first poop in the potty today!
	I know when to use toilet paper, but still need assistance.
	I can get a new roll of toilet paper and help replace the roll.
	I picked out my underwear at the store or I received my first pair today.
	I can tell the front from the back of my underwear.
	I can pull up my underwear or training pants by myself.
	I can stay dry with gentle reminders to go potty during the day.
	I can wear underwear when spending the day at home.
	I can wear underwear and stay dry on short outings.
	I used a public toilet.
	I can pee in the potty on a regular basis.
	I can do a bowel movement in the potty on a regular basis.
	I am starting to go potty all by myself without reminders.
	I often wake up in the morning with a dry diaper.
	I started night time/bed training.
	I keep my bed dry if I take a nap.
	I can keep my bed dry when sleeping most of the time.
	I am learning to wipe all by myself.
	I can wear underwear all the time! Hooray!

GOODBYE DIAPERS - 45 IDEAS!
What works for one child may not work for another.
Find some ideas that will help your child!

Attitude

1) Potty training can start at about 18 months when the body can physically control the necessary muscles. However, some children begin to train at three years old or later.

2) What no one ever told me #1: How long will it take? There are cases where potty training was completed in a day but in reality, regardless of initial training length, you will gently remind your child to go for the next year. It will be on your mind before car rides, trips to the park, walks, and other outings far from a potty.

3) What no one ever told me #2: What is the definition of "trained"? Parents would say their children were trained. I learned to ask for details. Did the children go by themselves? Did the parent remind them every hour and thus no accidents? (Some call this the parent being trained.) Did they wipe themselves? Did they sleep in diapers? Decide on your own definition and goals and confidently train your child!

4) When are children ready? Can they follow instructions? Have they shown an interest through actions or questions about the potty? Discuss independence in children's terms. Can they get dressed, feed themselves, brush their teeth, and clean up toys? Do they have daily patterns when they go/stay dry? Do they pause when they have a bowel movement? Do they tell you they have a messy diaper? Children do not have to do all of these things but training will go faster if they have some of these traits.

5) Focus patiently on five basic steps: removing pants, using toilet paper if needed, flushing, pulling up pants and washing hands. Keep childcare personnel, relatives, and babysitters informed on your child's progress and have them use your approach.

6) Is it easier in a certain season? In spring and summer children wear less making it easier to remove clothing and get to a sitting position fast. When spending long hours outside, place the potty in the yard. Fall and winter have the advantage of a dryer carpet as long pants absorb accidents. Plus, night training will then follow in summer, when our biological clock and summer pajamas make accidents a little easier to get up for and to handle. A second advantage is you are indoors more anyway. Who wants to spend their summers inside just to be near a toilet?

7) Take note of your child's daily patterns ahead of time. Encourage your child to go potty at these times. Some parents say easy no pressure reminders such as "Don't forget about the potty." Others do not remind but instead take their child to the bathroom when they feel their child will be able to go.

8) Do not get angry about accidents; praise enthusiastically for success. Be aware that accidents increase when children are sick or tired. I even kept track (a diary/chart) of accidents and successes. This helped me know we were making progress.

9) Some events can cause short-lived regression: your child has a cold, a new baby, a family issue such as moving to a new town or separation. Continue to encourage.

10) Some children love to flush; others fear "a part of them" is disappearing down the toilet. Many like to wave and call out, "Bye Bye Poo Poo!" Children are intrigued by the different smells, colors, shapes and sizes of their accomplishments in the toilet. Let them look. It is normal. Comments like, "Wow! Great job getting that one in there!" or "Pee ew! You're stinking it up - Let's wash hands and get out of here!" can make it fun. Your tone of voice is the key.

11) Choose words carefully when discussing bowel movements. "Big one" sounds better than "dirty" and say it with a smile. This reassures children they did nothing bad. Bowel control often comes first. Some potty resisters control bowels by waiting for a private place (corner, closet, etc.) to go in their pants! Try to see this as a positive - because they are controlling it.

Clothes

12) Use easy on and off pants. Avoid overalls, buttons and long t-shirts. Dresses may be faster for girls but have to be held high when sitting and underwear does not absorb much so prepare for a wet floor. Buy at least six pairs of underwear. Then buy three more, one size too big, to grow into and use for emergency. Larger sizes are easier to pull up and down. When pushing down and pulling up pants, instruct your child to bend his or her knees and to use one hand in front and one in back rather than side by side. As children increasingly wear underwear, their skin can become more prone to diaper rashes when accidents occur. Apply cream if needed.

13) You can train immediately in any of these: a bare bottom, diapers, pull-ups, plastic-wet pants over underwear, or underwear (thick or regular). Often parents start with one option and progress towards underwear. Diapers are cheaper than pull-ups and the tabs will re-stick a few times. Pull-ups (which tear down the sides for easy removal) sometimes retain moisture too well and your child does not feel wet. Try using underwear underneath the pull-ups. (My child insisted she was dry unless her legs got wet. Since the crotch of a pull up or plastic wet pants is usually dry on the outside, she would touch her crotch and say, "Dry Mama." She was right. For her - understanding wet underneath was difficult! We switched to train in underwear.)

14) If your child has pull-ups or underwear with a pattern all around and has trouble telling the front from the back, take a laundry pen and color a big star on the front center band. Instruct your child, "The star goes on your belly button" - problem solved! Of course your child, like my son, may now want a star on all underwear, even if there are no patterns, but this is no problem!

15) For soiled underwear, hold a clean part and shake in the toilet while flushing. The flushing force cleans a significant amount off and you can toss them in your wash. Adding ¼ cup of white vinegar to washes neutralizes accidents and helps cleaning.

Equipment / Training

16) Teach an understanding of "feels wet vs. dry." Use props such as a wet wash cloth. Start teaching body parts and words you will use for urination and bowel movements.

17) Have a good footstool to wash hands at the sink. The footstool also helps maintain stability when bearing down during a poop on the adult toilet. Try letting your child sit sideways or backwards on the toilet. Comfort is a key to relaxation and success.

18) Have a sturdy potty seat on the floor or toilet. You may want two seats if you have more than one bathroom. Adding water to a floor potty will make emptying deposits easier. It also helps with odor control. Potty seats are NOT all the same:

    a. The soft squishy musical potty seat, sits on the adult toilet and plays music as long as your child will sit. This encourages a longer sitting time.

    b. Another musical potty plays a song only when your child is successful. This potty has a special sensor to register moisture contact.

    c. The Flip-n-Flush potty permanently attaches to the toilet. You flip it down over the adult seat for child use and later flip up for adult use. It eliminates lifting potty seats on and off the toilet. See http://www.flipnflush.com/.

    d. Converting seats are used on the floor and later on the adult toilet. Handles will aid when bearing down. Soft cushion seats do not feel cold. Some styles have another added feature: the lid closes to become a stool to wash hands.

19) Some parents have success moving the potty to where their child plays until their child gains confidence and expertise. You can purchase a foldable privacy screen decorated as a bathroom called a Potty Surround. This scaled down bathroom can be moved from room to room along with your potty. See http://www.ablebaby.com/.

20) Parents do have success in training completely in one day. Often the child is older, follows directions well and is bare bottom. This method usually involves increasing fluid intake (water, juice, milk etc.) to increase the need to use the potty. You spend the day in the kitchen or bathroom with a plan of spending an hour teaching a doll to go potty, then playing toys and games with few distractions, gentle reminders to go and no rug. You must have a schedule where you can devote 6-8 hours or a day to sit by your child. Be sure your child has shown readiness signs and you are both psychologically ready. Increased fluid intake can also result in increased accidents and mentally turn a child away from training. If you try this method, I just caution that you cease as soon as one of you (yourself or your child) becomes frustrated. You can always try it again another day and you will both be happier you did.

21) Many parents have great success in training only part of the day. I trained my second child only during the mornings and in the afternoons we put the diaper back on and focused on other things. We took it very slow.

22) Your child's attitude determines the speed needed for each training stage. Let your child play with the potty, sit with clothes on, and sit bare-bottom to get used to the potty feel. Use the potty on the floor, then on the toilet and later, use the toilet alone.

23) The sound of running tap water may help your child relax and go. Also try letting your child play with special toys in a pan or basin of warm water while sitting bare-bottom on the potty. (A dinner tray can hold the pan if needed.) You are having fun and the sensation of the water on the fingers often helps the child relax and go.

24) Let the child go bare-bottom if possible or even naked. Closely watch for accidents.

25) Read potty-related books any time to introduce the potty idea and continue reading them while training. Also, reading books (potty-related or just a favorite) on the potty will add to sitting time, relax your child, and increase chances of success.

26) Encourage copying / imitating by having a sibling, friend, or yourself demonstrate. A medicine dropper (well hidden) behind an animal or doll also demonstrates well.

27) Play potty while training a stuffed animal or doll. Use your child's future underwear on the animal. Because the underwear is big, it will be easier for your child to teach pulling pants down and up. Play house and pretend with your child. You be animal's mommy. Feed the animal, make it run to the potty, pull pants down, sit, maybe read a book to it, praise it for trying/accomplishing, wipe, pull pants up, flush and wash hands. Play again. Let your child be Mommy and take the animal through the steps with you offering corrections if needed. Repeat. Devoting time here with excessive repetition may bore you but provides great instruction for your child. Review our tips for things to spice it up: accidents, songs, rules, or visiting.

28) Motivate them!

   a. Go to the store and let them pick their own special underwear to keep dry.
   b. Some parents use reward motivation (positive reinforcement) for any performance and others reward only for bowel movements. Rewards could be: praise, a hug, a potty success sticker chart (order ours at the end of this book), special underwear, a snack (raisins, nuts, or crackers) or candy.
   Note: Some parents regret food motivation, especially if you have siblings.
   c. Try adding blue food dye to the toilet. Let your child turn it green by going!
   d. Let your child take control by picking the day potty training starts. Use a calendar to remind it is coming. Have a "used the last diaper celebration party" or make a big deal out of throwing it away. Be sure not to buy more.
   e. If applicable, stress they can go to pre-school, swimming, etc. once trained.

29) Set your watch or kitchen timer to beep every hour. Take your child when it beeps. It reminds you how long it has been since the last trip and can be fun for your child. My second child loved to scream, "Beep beep, gotta go!" It also avoided accidents by reminding me while I was cooking, folding laundry or focusing on another task.

30) Sing a silly song rhyme made up to any tune. Words I sang with my daughter are: "Gotta go potty, gotta go potty, gotta go potty, cause that's when you gotta go!"

31) Many parents first train boys sitting. Splash-guards are not needed if boys lean forward. When standing, try putting a target in the toilet to aim at. Targets could be: a piece of cereal, a toilet paper square colored with a red bull's-eye (it will sink when hit), some colored dish soap (see if he can make bubbles) or you can purchase little tissue animals to aim at. (A variation game is seeing how close he can get to the rim without getting outside. Have cleanser and sponge handy.) You can also buy a green light to attach to the toilet, which turns on when you lift the seat. Besides the night benefits, some boys become intrigued about trying to go and are reminded to put the seat down (turn the light off). It never hurts to train this habit early.

32) Race with your child to see who can get to the potty first. Guess who wins?

33) Try gradually easing into a set of rules/daily routine with no pressure. Most rules will be called it "trying to sit." Each try should be no more that 5 minutes and the golden rule is "we must sit even if we do not go." Offer praise for sitting even if there is no production. With enough rules, eventually there is little space in the day for accidents. Add these rules as soon as you can, but only with no resistance:

    a. We always try to sit before getting in the tub for a bath.
    b. We always try to sit before a meal and again after a meal.
    c. We always try to sit before going outside, in the car or for a walk.
    d. We always try to sit before sleeping (nap or bed) and after waking up.
    e. We wear diapers for long car rides, library story time or grocery store (times to avoid accidents). Children accept and understand simple explanations for a diaper "switch." They are not confused about switching for bed, right?

34) Gently increasing daily drinks (juices are popular) creates more opportunities to practice using the potty. You want to increase fruits (don't forget raisins and prunes) and vegetables too. Salads, with the oil from the dressing, are a great help to keep stools soft, promote easy/painless passages, and help prevent (what is a common problem) a child having stomach cramps from withholding a bowel movement. Withholding Solutions: (Some of these ideas can be used for urination training too.)

    a. *Try to determine the cause:* Visit your pediatrician to see if it is a physical or medical problem. Is it a power struggle/battle of the wills between you and your child? Is it forgetfulness - a desire to continue playing also referred to as laziness? Is it a fear of falling in, fear of a painful movement, fear of having an accident and displeasing you? Is it a combination of these?
    b. *Bath:* For every accident, try requiring a quick bath with slightly cooler than warm water temperature. You might say, "Yes, the water is a little cold. We will be quick, so we can play. If you use the potty next time, it will not be messy and we can skip a bath. You do a great job. You can do it next time!"
    c. *Clean Up*: Emptying soiled diapers/underwear into the potty in front of your child may reinforce the idea of where poop belongs. Gentle reminders while doing this also help. Some parents have tried having their child clean up accidents in the hope that if they have to do the clean up work, it will motivate them to use the potty instead. This is for a capable child who can rinse underwear, put wet ones in the laundry, wash/bathe, and change to dry clothes. It requires supervision, help, and ends with a bath/soapy hand wash.
    d. *Set Times*: Try a daily routine for three weeks or more with set times to sit. Sitting for only 10 minutes after meals works well. Have really special toys or books for use only in these sittings. The goal is loss of pain association, reduction in fear, and some deposits. This method may be combined with daily doses (ask your pediatrician for the correct amount) of mineral oil.
    e. *Scissors*: Offer the diaper if your child will wear it sitting on the potty and go. Meanwhile your child will wear underwear. He or she will be getting used to going in a sitting position. Once this is going smoothly, discreetly cut a hole in the bottom of the diaper. Continue to cut larger holes each time. (Children soon see they are going potty and do not need the diaper after all.)
    f. *Back Off:* Wait until your child is older. It is most important to get the colon to a normal size and go regularly. Calmly change soiled underwear and remind how good daily relief feels. Do not buy any more diapers.

Bed Training

35) Begin bed training after your child wakes up dry some mornings. Start training during naps if your child still takes one. Protective wet pads go on top of the fitted bed sheet. Most accidents stay on the pad and are replaced without changing sheets.

36) Limiting fluid intake prior to sleeping may help. (My son's last drink was at dinner.)

37) Try letting you child sleep with a bare bottom. Boys can wear large nightshirts. The idea is there is nothing for the child to go "into" as the bottom is no longer wrapped.

38) Try waking your child before you go to bed (even carry your child to the potty) to try and go. Your child may not even remember it the next day and can be proud of a dry bed. I have memories squatting in a hug with my son on the potty half asleep - yet he still did go. If there is any resistance, let your child sleep, try again tomorrow.

39) Wake your child five minutes earlier (than your child's normal waking time) and go directly to the potty. I even carried her there in a big good morning hug as I met with little resistance that way. Then go back and praise for a dry bed (if applicable).

40) There is a bedwetting alarm available. The alarm sounds upon detecting moisture on the pad attached waking your child who then proceeds to the toilet. The expectation is that over time (90 days) your child will be conditioning his/her own internal clock.

Public / Traveling

41) Public toilets - ALWAYS be with your child. Use the larger handicap restroom.

42) Let your child see and use different bathrooms: friends, libraries, and restaurants.

43) Wipe the toilet with toilet paper and let your child sit directly on the seat or put toilet paper or toilet covers (provided in some restrooms) on the seat. Let your child sit on the paper. Catalogs also have foldable traveling potty seats you carry in your purse.

44) Positioning / Balance: Those little fingers just want to grab under the seat for balance! Instead, your child can hold on to you for balance if you stand directly in front of your sitting child and instruct him or her to hold your legs. This is also a great position for assisting with wiping, as you can easily reach behind your child and he or she can lean against your legs for support.

45) Travel and visit with spare clothing and if you have the car space, bring the potty. Line it with a plastic bag and you can stop anywhere on the road to let your child go. Remove the plastic bag, tie it up and drop it in a roadside trash. Line the potty again and you are set. You can also purchase an inflatable potty, which also uses the same idea with plastic bags. Be sure your bags are sealed. On an extremely windy day, I don't think I ever laughed so hard watching my husband, who was the one emptying, struggle in the wind with a leaky bag! Despite his smiling too - it really was no fun!

For more order forms and toilet training supplies, please visit our website:
http://tracytrends.com/

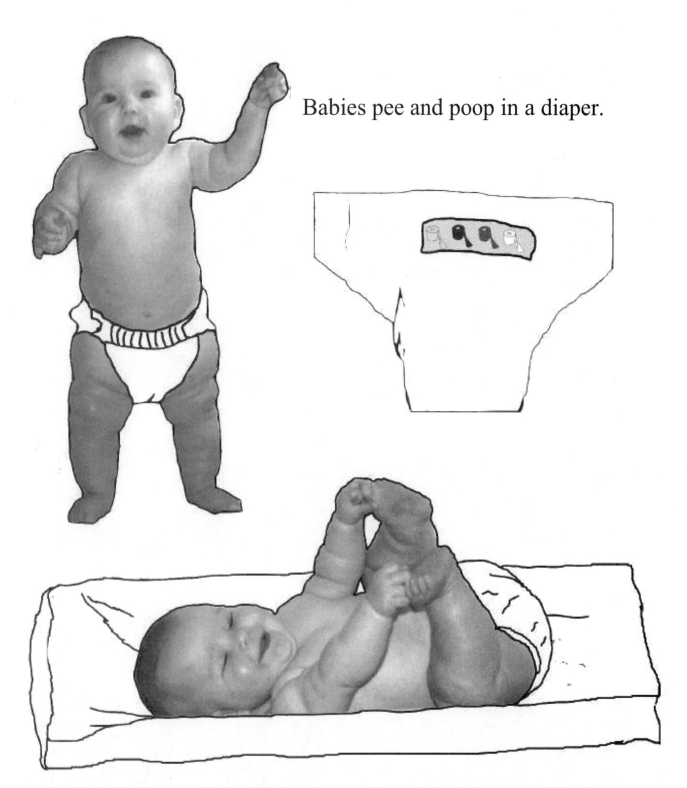

Babies pee and poop in a diaper.

Babies lay on a changing pad or table while Mom and Dad help put on a clean diaper. Color the diapers different colors. Color the changing pad too.

These are things we eat and drink. Color them.
When you eat and drink, soon you will have to pee and poop.

Animals also eat and drink. Soon they have to pee and poop too.

Color the dog food different colors.

We have a special place to pee and poop.
Adults go in the toilet and toddlers go in a potty.

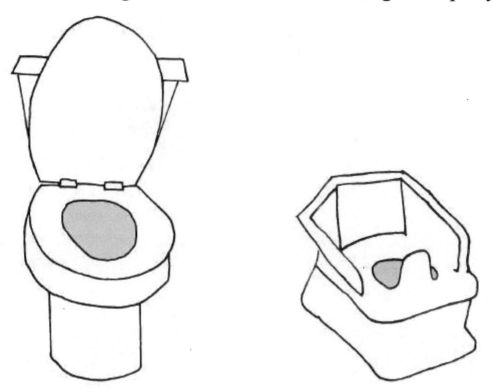

Decorate the toilet for Mom. Decorate the potty for you.

Cats also have a special place to pee and poop.
Color the cat's box your favorite color.

I tried sitting on the potty with my clothes on to see how it feels!

My sister tried it too!
After you color, see if you can sit on yours.

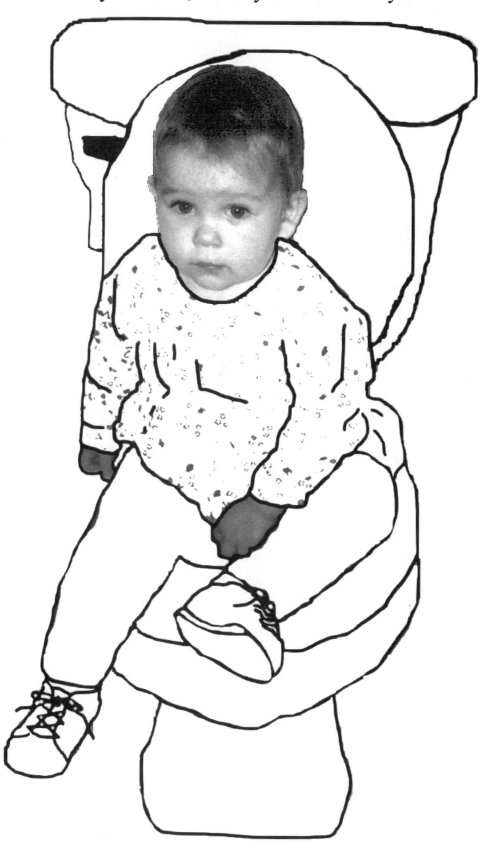

Grandma's potty might have looked like these when she was a little girl. Color one pink, one yellow and one orange.

When Grandpa was a boy, his potty might have looked like these. Color one red, one blue and one green. Color my clothes too.

This old potty has a duck on it.
Decorate it with your crayons!

This old potty is made of metal and has a tray. Feel something metal in your house. Imagine how cold it was to sit on metal! Would you want to sit on metal? Not me!

We love to sing songs on the potty. This potty has a funny shape and sensor that makes music <u>only</u> when you go. Sing a song while you color this page. Then go sing the same song while sitting on your potty.

I can do a lot by myself. I can feed myself, brush my own teeth and put away toys. I can almost get dressed. Now, I am learning to go potty by myself too. I am not a baby anymore! Can you do some of these things too?

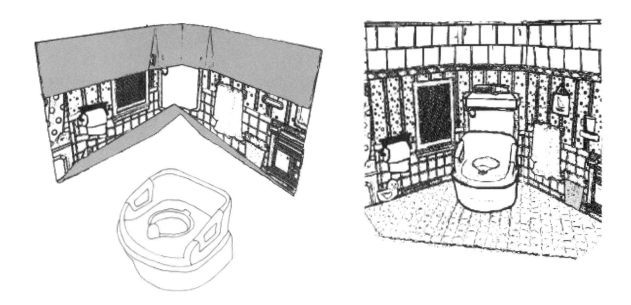

My cardboard "Potty Surround" folds up to be used in any room. I add my potty and I have my own little bathroom/privacy screen. Now I do not have to run far!

Connect the diamonds to make a potty.

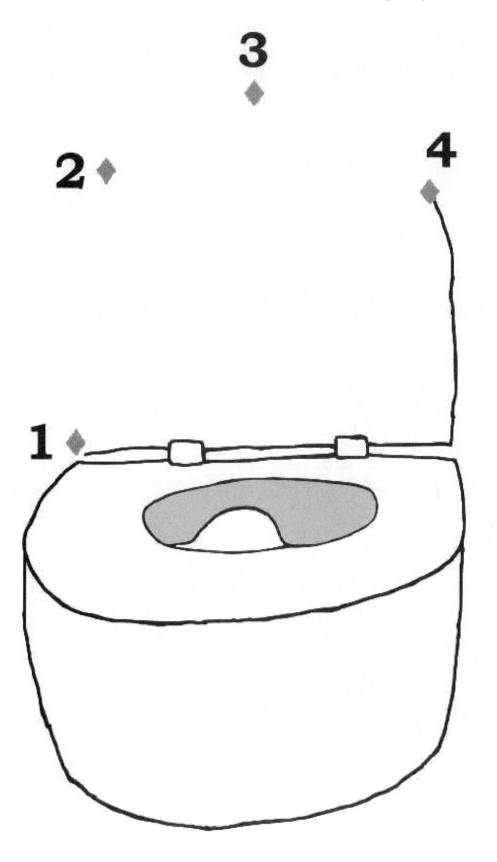

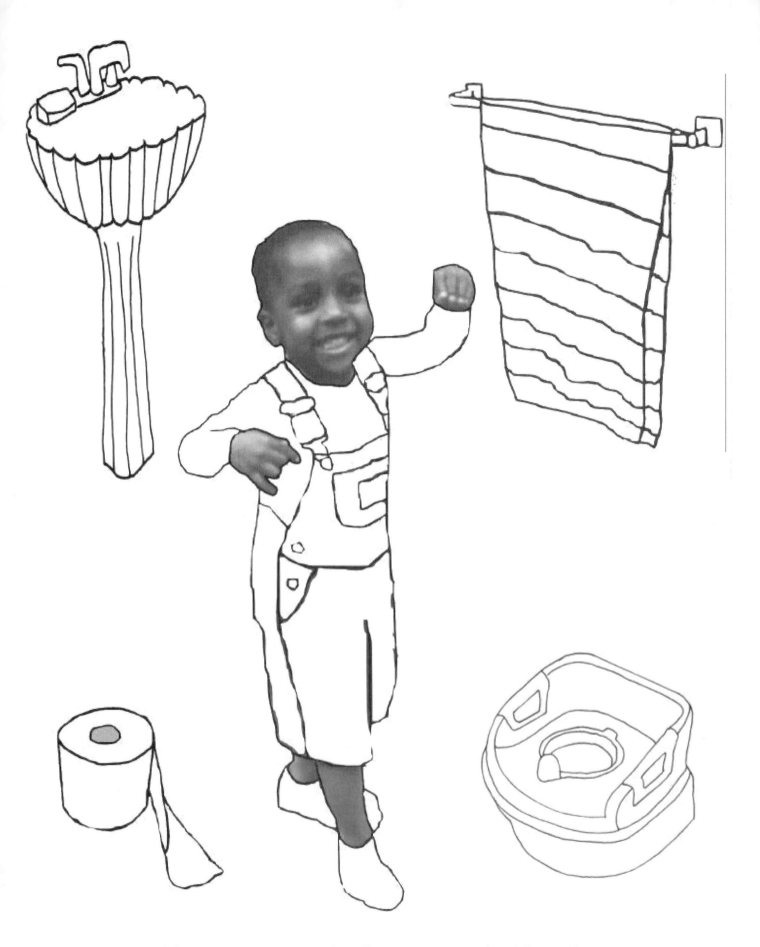

This potty goes on the floor next to the big toilet.

When I get bigger, my
potty comes apart and I can
use it on the big toilet.

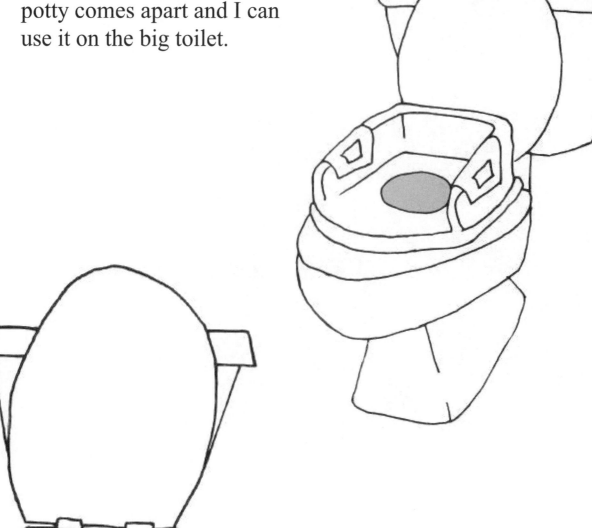

When I am even bigger, I get to
use the big toilet alone!

We use toilet paper to wipe. We do not want poop or pee pee left on our body. Color each roll a different color.

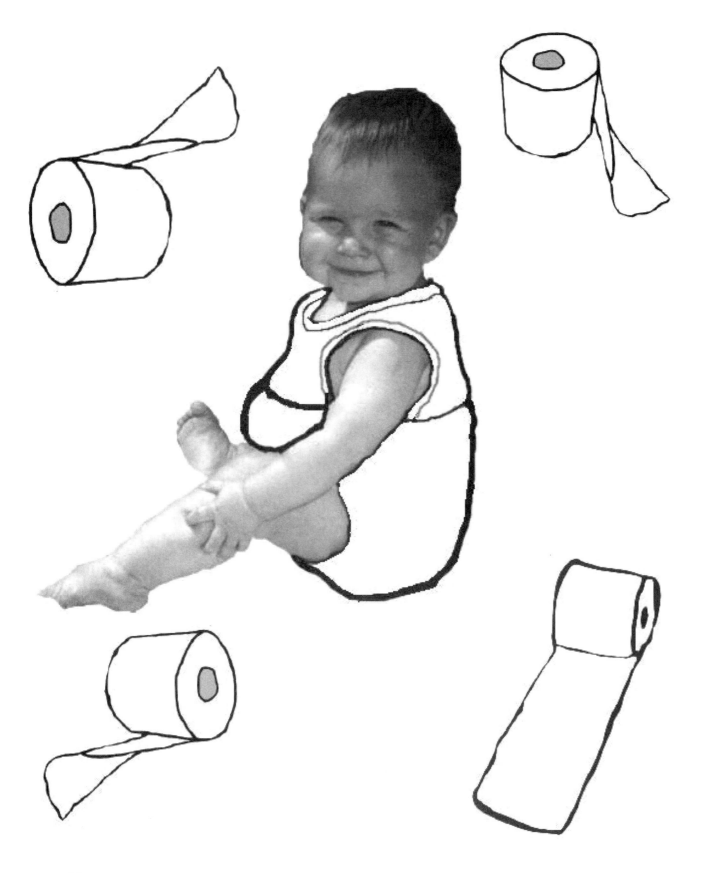

We wash our hands every time we go potty. This makes sure our hands have no pee pee or poop on them. After you color this page, go to the sink, wash your hands and see if you can make lots of bubbles with your soap.

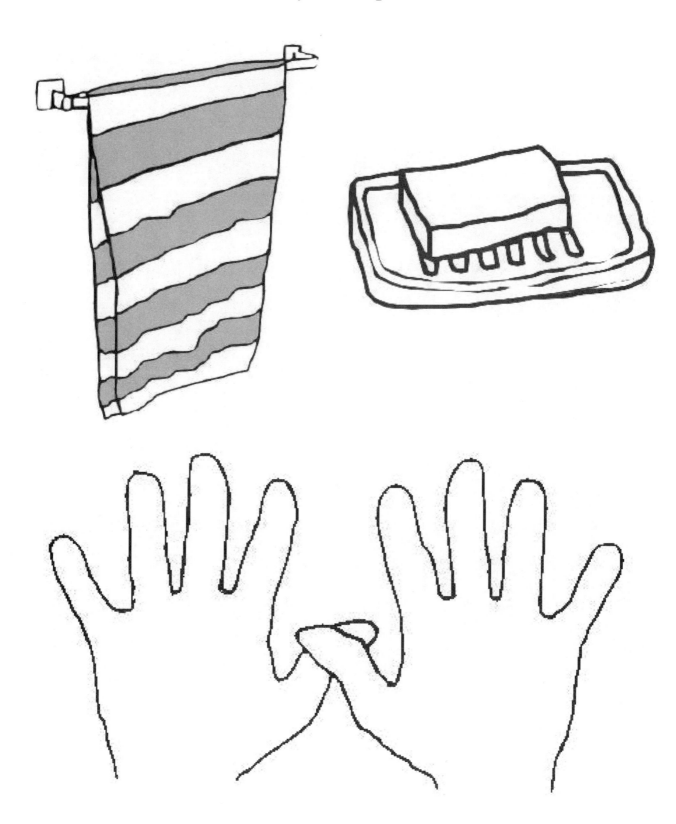

Shopping for toilet paper is a lot of fun!
Color the rolls different colors.

Circle the potty that is different.
Color the three potties that are the same.

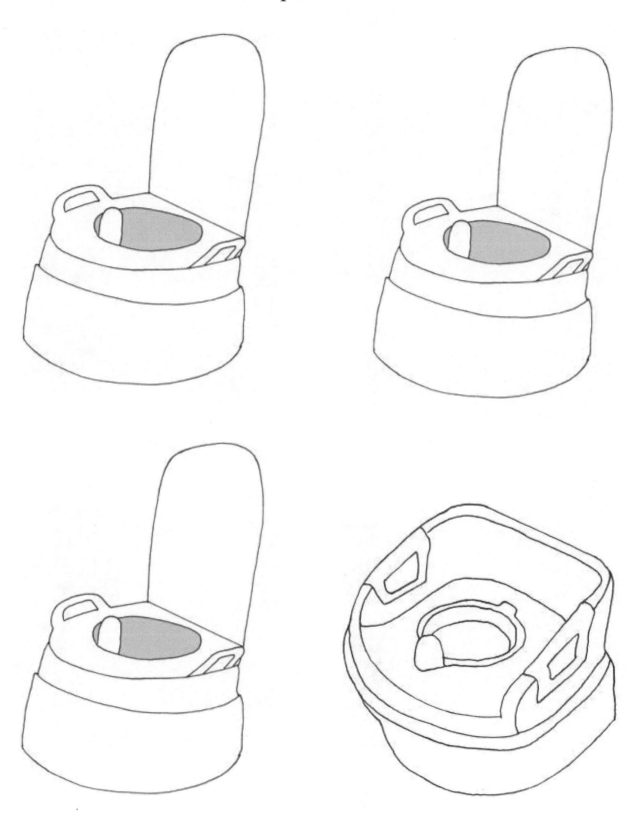

I receive a sticker when I go potty! Do you get a reward? A hug? A treat? A special story? Circle the sticker you would like and color my dress and shoes.

I love to flush! Do you look to see what you made? Lots of children do. Poops come in all shapes, colors and sizes. It's fun to look … but not fun to smell…

Bye Bye POO POO!

What comes next? Connect
each little girl to a potty.
(All answers are correct)

Oops! I had an accident! Have you ever had an accident? It's OK, my Mom helps me change my clothes.

Circle the object that does not belong.
Color the objects that belong in a bathroom.

Draw a line to help Michael get to the potty.

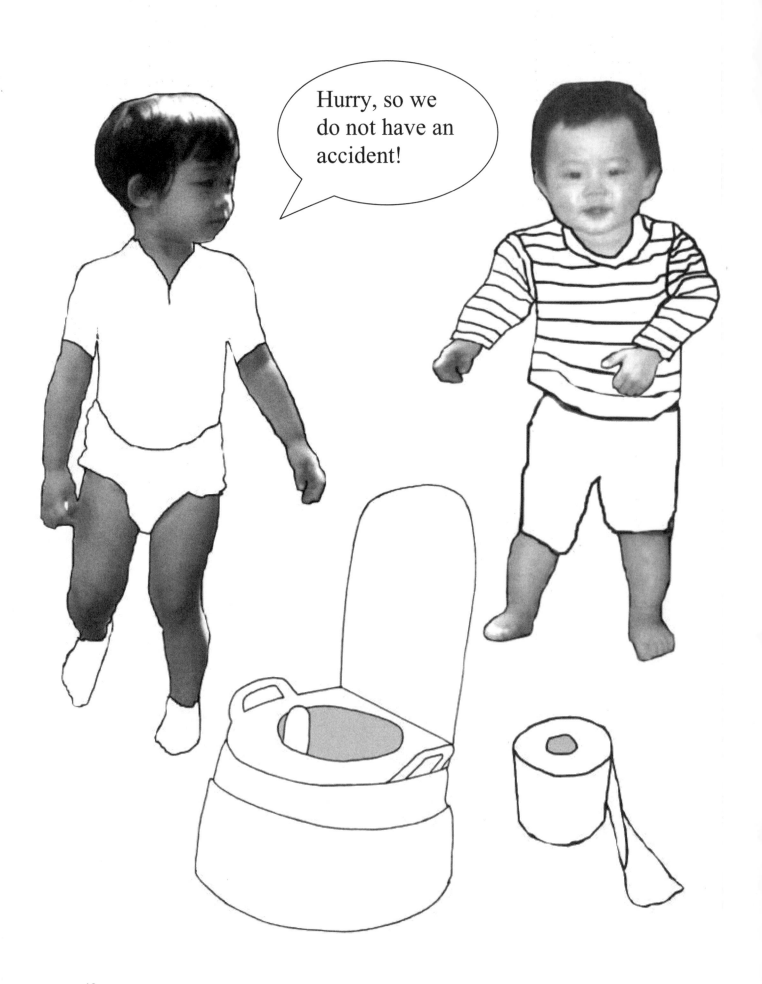

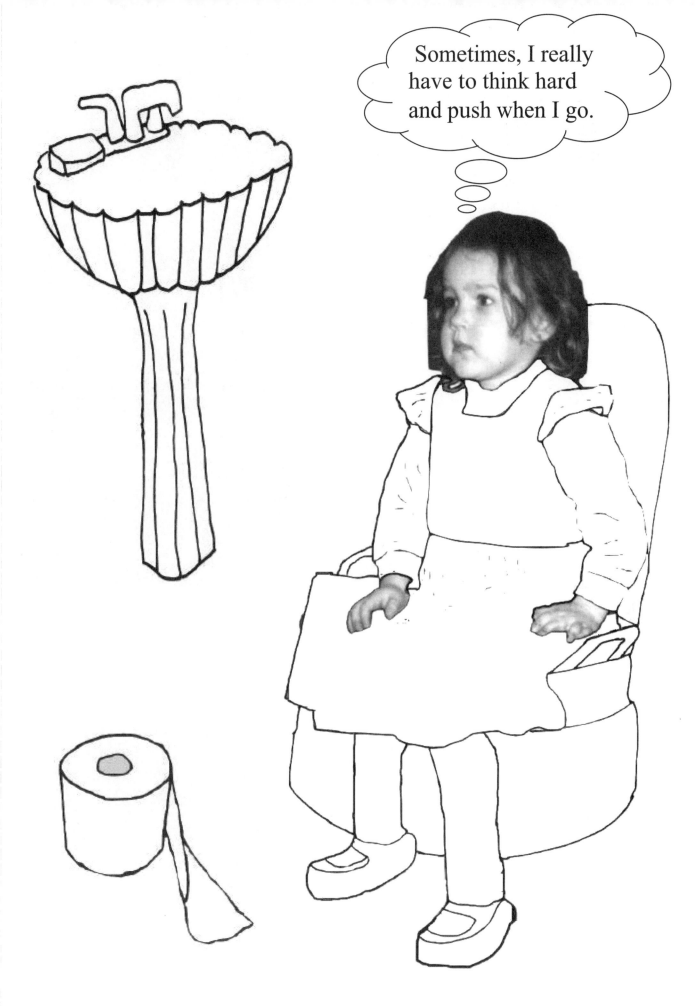

1

2

3

4

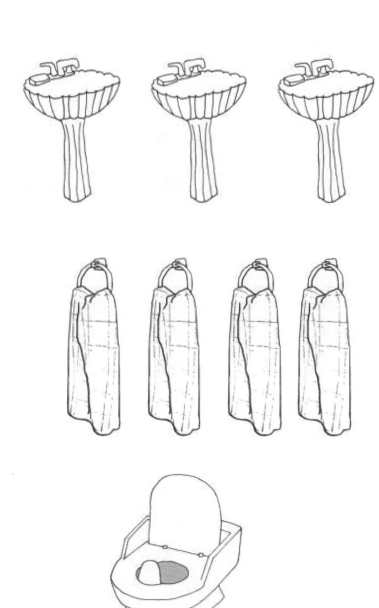

Look at the number. Find the set that matches.
Draw a line to connect them.

Mommy puts a bag over the toilet roll so I can have books ready to read when I go potty. Color the page and then pick a book to read on the potty with your mom.

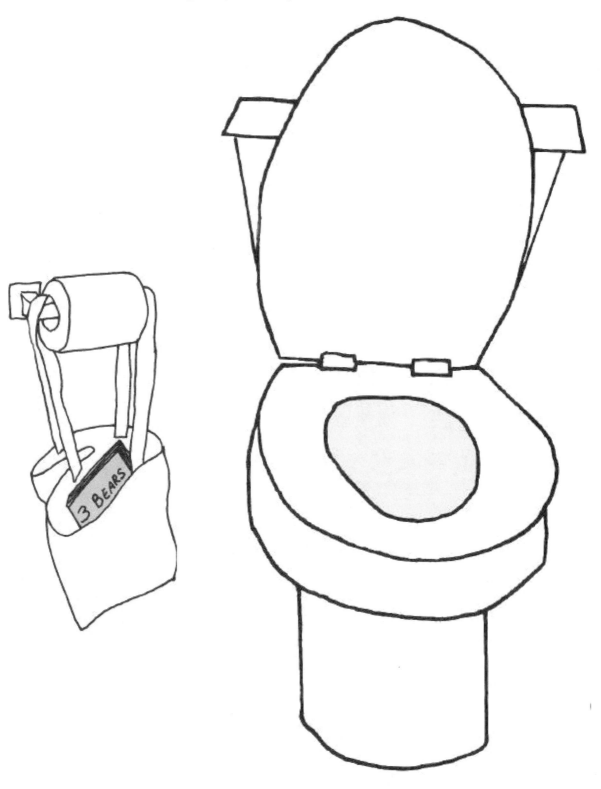

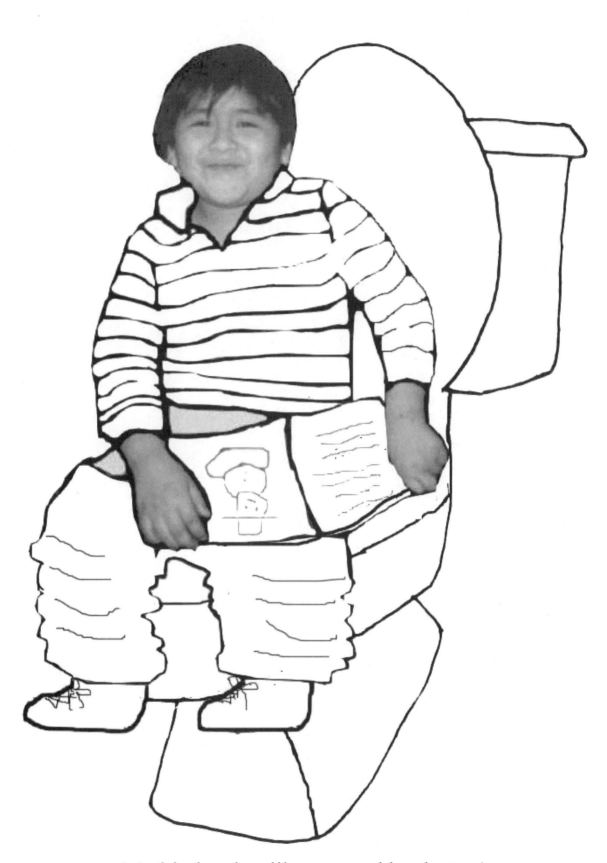

My big brother likes to read books too!

Circle the potty you would like to use. Color it your favorite
color. Then color the others.

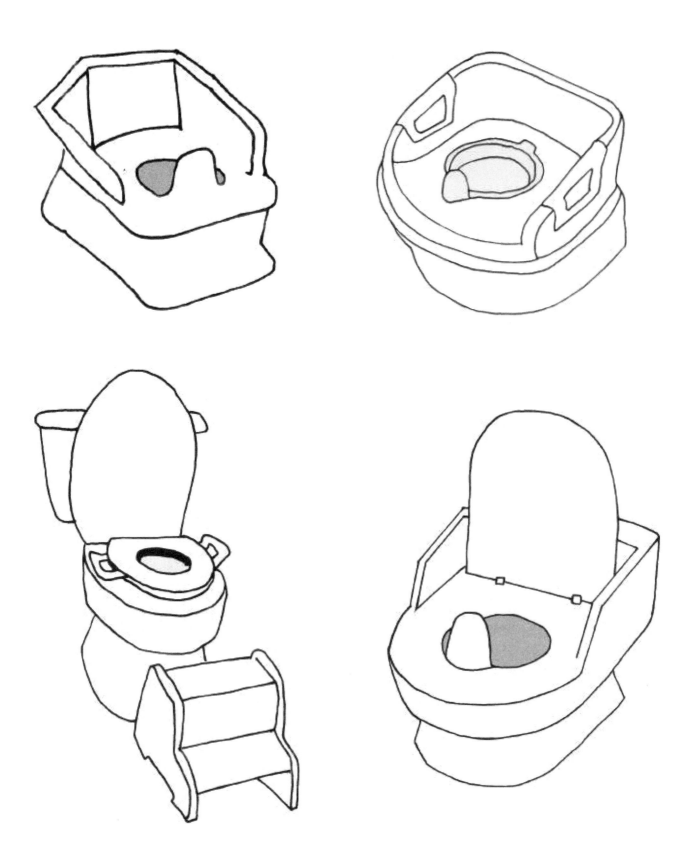

Do you take your potty in the car when you go visiting or traveling on long trips? It is cleaner than public bathrooms and is great when there is no bathroom.

Draw a line to connect each boy to an underwear.
(All answers are correct)

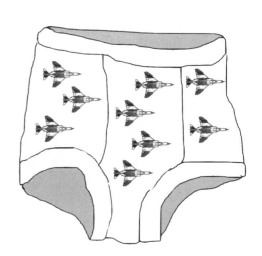

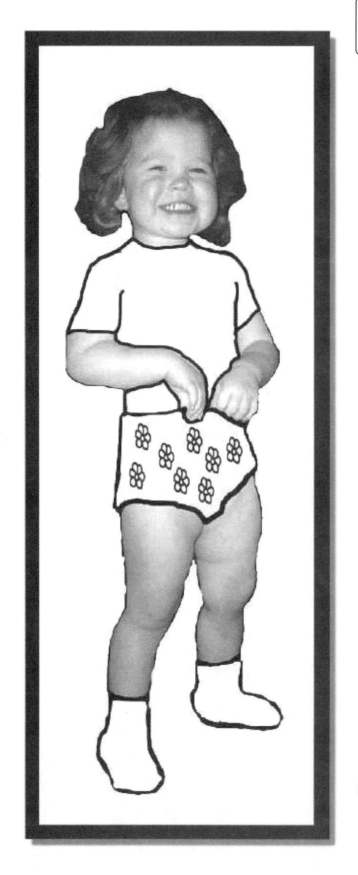
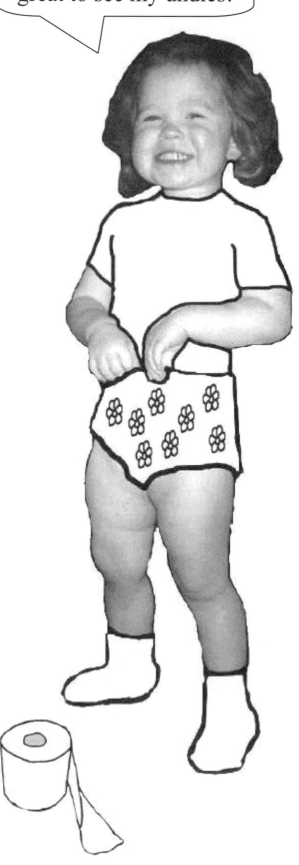

P O T T Y

Tracy Trends
Tissue

Trace the word and color the picture.

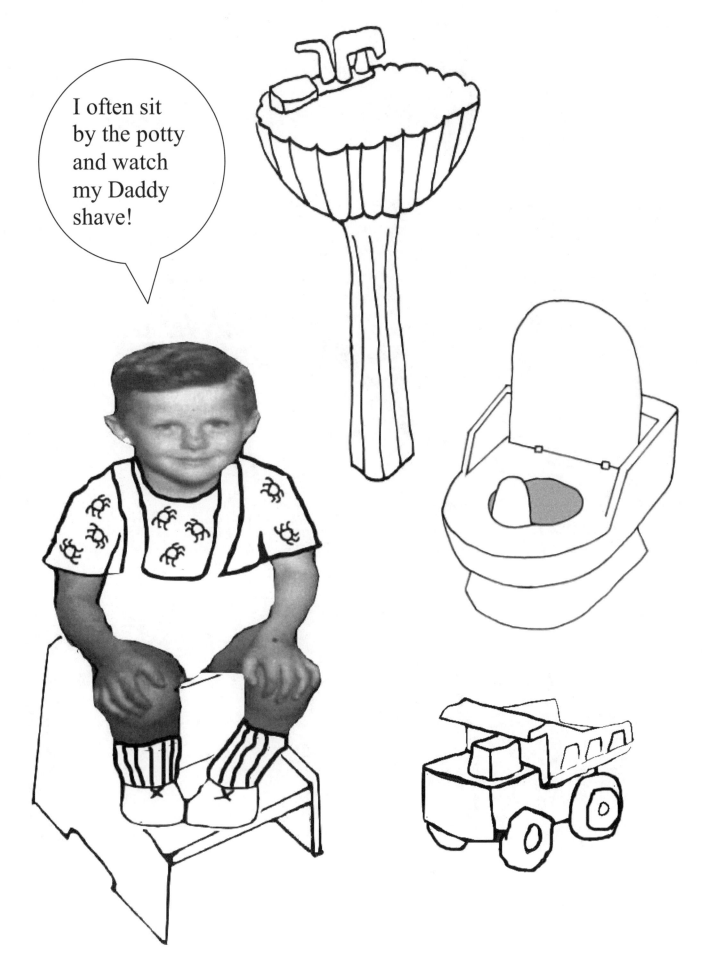

Do you wake up with a dry diaper?
Soon you can try to wear underwear to bed.

Connect the dots to make a potty. What goes in a potty?
Draw a line connecting the potty to things that go inside it.

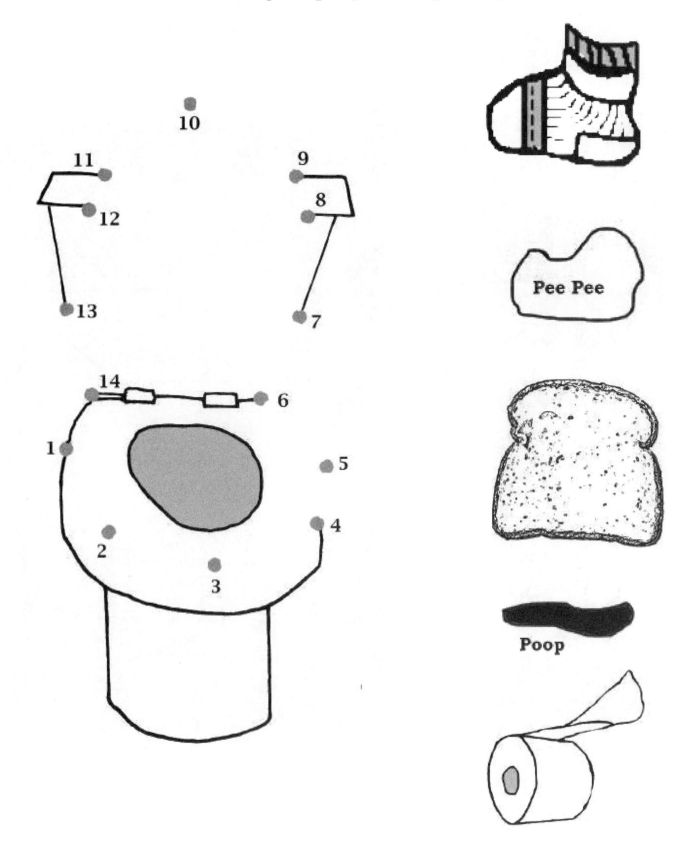

Pee Pee

Poop

Circle the underwear you would like to wear and color it.
Then color the others for friends!

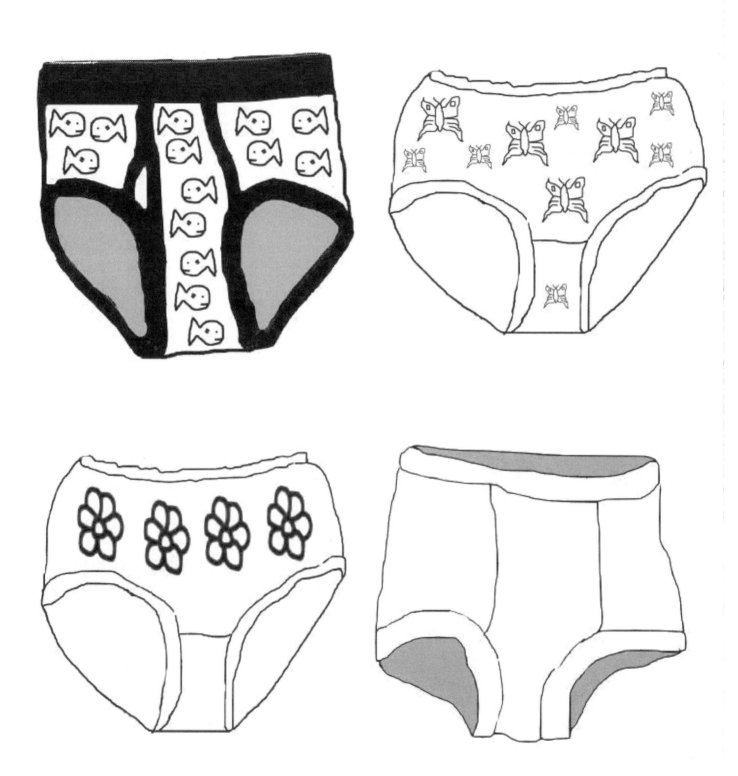

I am a
Potty Graduate!

(Place child's photo here.)

This certificate is presented to

_____

Age_____ on _____ (date)

In recognition of great efforts
made toward potty training!

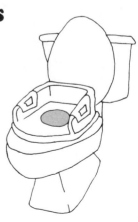

TracyTrends.com
Encouraging spending time with children.

Other Parent Potty Training Helpers
By TracyTrends.com

My Potty Calendar

This well planned calendar tracks successes and accidents, attitude, memorable experiences, training method, and more. Each month has colorful potty related photos to spur your child's interest. Plus, there are 63 stickers to place on the calendar as they are accomplished. You choose what month it starts!

My Potty Reward Stickers and Chart for Boys and for Girls

Motivate and reward your child using full color stickers. The 126 reward stickers found inside these booklets will last a long time and are great for positive reinforcement. Each sticker is a one-inch circle of a colorful potty related subject. After successful potty attempts place one on your child's shirt or use the progress chart provided. No repetition - all stickers are different!

(ISBN 13: 978-0-9708226-8-0)   (ISBN: 978-0-9708226-7-3)

QUICK ORDER FORM

Check your local bookstore,
order at our website: http://www. TracyTrends.com
Or mail this form to:

**TracyTrends
C/O T. Foote
27 West 86 Suite 17B
New York, NY 10024**

TracyTrends!

Unused items are returnable within 30 days for a full refund of the purchase price - no questions asked.

Customer Information (Please Print)

Name: _____

Daytime Phone: _____

Address: _____

_____

_____

E-mail: _____

Shipping Information (if different)

Name: _____

Daytime Phone: _____

Address: _____

_____

_____

Item Description	Quantity	Price Each	Sub Total
My Potty Activity Book +45 Toilet Training Tips: Parent/Child Interaction with Coloring and Creative Fun ISBN 13: 97-0-9708226-0-4		$ 9.95	$
My Potty Reward Stickers for Boys: 126 Stickers and Chart to Motivate Toilet Training ISBN 13: 978-0-9708226-8-0		$ 7.95	$
My Potty Reward Stickers for Girls: 126 Stickers and Chart to Motivate Toilet Training ISBN 13: 978-0-9708226-7-3		$ 7.95	$
My Potty Calendar (a 12 month calendar for monitoring progress) Starting Month/Year: _____ (example: Nov / 2001)		$ 12.95	$
	Sub Total:		$
Shipping: US: $4.50 first item $2.00 each additional item International: $9.00 first item, $5.00 each additional item	Shipping (at left)		$
	Total US dollars:		$

Payment Method:

In US Dollars payable to TracyTrends:
Money Order: _____ Cashier/Personal Check:_____
Credit Card: Visa _____ Mastercard _____

Number: _____ Exp Date: _____

Signature: _____